INSIDE
TURTLE'S SHELL

To Ms. Koenig
and her writers and
illustrators —
Happy Reading!
Happy Writing!
Happy Drawing!
Joanne Ryder
1990

INSIDE TURTLE'S SHELL

and Other Poems of the Field by Joanne Ryder

Drawings by Susan Bonners

Macmillan Publishing Company

New York

Macmillan Publishing Company
866 Third Avenue, New York, N.Y. 10022
Collier Macmillan Canada, Inc.

Printed in the United States of America
10   9   8   7   6   5   4   3

Library of Congress Cataloging in Publication Data
Ryder, Joanne.
Inside turtle's shell, and other poems of the field.

Summary: A collection of poems that portray the meadow
and its creatures from morning till night.
1. Animals—Juvenile poetry.   2. Meadows—Juvenile
poetry.   3. Children's poetry, American.   [1. Meadows—
Poetry.   2. Meadow animals—Poetry.   3. American poetry]
I. Bonners, Susan, ill.   II. Title.
PS3568.Y399Is   1985   811'.54   84-833
ISBN 0-02-778010-4

For Meredith
with joy and love
—J. R.

INSIDE
TURTLE'S SHELL

The morning fog
fills in the spaces
between grass and bush and pond.
The meadow is quiet.
Everyone is alone
thinking,
*Everyone is gone
but me.*

Tiny mice
welcome Mama,
her fat cheeks
full of breakfast.

The sun
makes its way
through the grass stems,
waking turtle
so old
if he could count,
he wouldn't count
this sunrise.

Rather, he opens his box
sticking his fat legs outside
as if to think,
Again?
        Ahhhhhhhhh!

From some tall grass
a meadow mouse
leaps up
to feel the morning
empty
all around her.

Bundles of seeds
perch
on tall bare stalks
that only last month
spread wings
of white and yellow.

But the morning glories
wake up the old stone wall
with blueness,
untwisting and blooming
for just one day—
today.

The last berries
turn
eat-me-red.

Their bushes
droop
with gray
sparrows.

Small bodies
wear small paths
among the weeds.
Some hungry one
leaps over turtle
and takes
a different path.

Creeping
through a tunnel
just his size,
turtle keeps on
and finds
the new round
mushrooms first.

Bumblebee hides
till the hot sun
warms her motor
and she leaps high
into a sky
buzzing
with fat furry friends.

Black snake
slides up
stealing
the sitting rock's
sun.

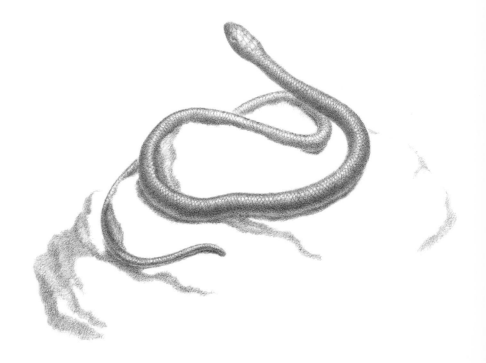

Today
the sun warms
a small egg
underground
and the new one
inside
feels the warmth,
knows she's ready
for changes.

Her fierce legs
kick and kick
tearing the wall
around her,
pushing her
outside
into the dark
into the soft earth
that holds her
that hides her.

But not for long.
She digs and digs
with new sharp claws
up and up
to the warmth
calling her.

At last,
she pushes up the lid
of her dark world
and sees
brown and green
red and gold
moving
in brightness
all around her.

Small turtle
blinks and blinks
then takes her first step
into her first day.

Fox
forgets
the tree trunk
isn't empty.

Downwind
everybody knows
skunk is angry.

Someone shakes turtle
inside his box
and leaves him
in the grass
unopened.

Blackbird's shadow
glides across the pond
chasing
sixty silver fish.

Frog waits
near the shore,
watching.
He breathes.
The water ripples.
He waits.

A shiny fly
buzzes
over the ripples.
Below,
fish stops
waiting
and leaps
high—
surprising
the fly,
surprising
frog.

Frog sings so pretty,
fox comes to listen.

Where's that frog now?

Up
from the deep
mud
comes a trail
of tiny bubbles.
Someone is hiding.
Who?

Even old catfish
asleep in the deep
hears tadpole's new song:
Oh, legs
Oh, my legs
        legs
        legs
        LEGS!

A long flapping V
settles on the pond
honking
resting
eating the sweet grasses.

Their visit over,
the wild geese rise
climbing stairs
no one can see.

Stalking the field
on tall thin legs,
crow stops and watches
someone new and fearless
creep toward him.
Crow stretches his wings
as if to greet a friend
and swoops,
his beak wide open.

Nearby,
heavy footsteps
crinkle the grass
and crow flees upward
leaving
his tiny lunch behind.

Small turtle
now knows
a new thing:
Watch out for crows!

Come!
See New Places!
FLY!!
No Wings Needed!

Many-legged creepers
and silky seeds
let go
     and
         sail   away
on the wind's promises.

A cold wind
stirs
the feathers
the fur
of finches
of mice
whispering,
winter is coming.

The finches
start singing
of sunnier places
but the mice—
making warm nests
underground—
do not hear them.

Ant
sighs
and climbs
over the rock in her path
tickling
turtle.

Small white bird
races with the clouds
and wins.

Dragonfly
darts closer and closer
to the gray twig
that is lizard.
Who sees the storm clouds
creep behind them?

Crackling on the stones,
the rain pounces
and the gray twig twitches.
A lizard breath later,
dragonfly dances
above the stone wall
above the short reach
of lizards and twigs.

Rain
bends
the tall grass
making
bridges
for ant.

Something angry
beats and beats
against
small turtle's shell.
She runs
under the sitting rock
away from the rain.

———

Turtle wanders
through the wetness
until it's time
to go inside
and listen
to his old friend
rain whisper,
sleep, sleep, sleep.

Turtle dreams
he is young
hunting in a wood
of tall trees,
so many trees
only the birds
could see
the wide blue sky.
Everyone was hidden
in the dark cool world
under the leaves
under the trees.

And turtle dreams
of the days
the tall trees fell
and he hid in his shell
each time
the ground shook.

But that was long ago,
nearly a hundred years.
Only turtle
remembers
the cool darkness of trees.

In the rain
toad sits alone,
eyes open, mouth closed
drinking the warm drops
through his skin.

Pawprints
in the wet ground
leave
a picture
of fox.

When the air
is silent and dry once more,
heads
tucked under wings and shells
pop out.
Damp soggy bodies
shake off
wetness.
Some move toward supper.
Some move toward home.

Only the long pink worms wait,
wriggling on the muddy ground
hoping their flooded cellars
will dry
before robin finds them.

A thousand
hidden musicians
play
a goodbye tune,
a cricket march
for the setting sun.

So busy
watching a fly,
small turtle
does not see
night come.

The sun
and the pond
disappear.
Over so soon,
she sighs,
and tucks herself
inside the darkness
she will
always call
home.

Patches of blackness
blot out the stars
for a moment, then pass.
High-flying songbirds
follow a pathway
in the sky
north to south.

Up from the grass
to the uppermost twigs
the field's singers stir
feeling the call:
now, now, now, now
summer is over
now, now, now, now
till they burst
from the bushes
to fly high
in the night.

Far below,
a young rabbit
stretches to hear
their short farewell song.
When it is over,
he hops off
into the quietness
that will last
until spring.

When the night ones come,
the meadow moves
with shadows
seeking shadows.

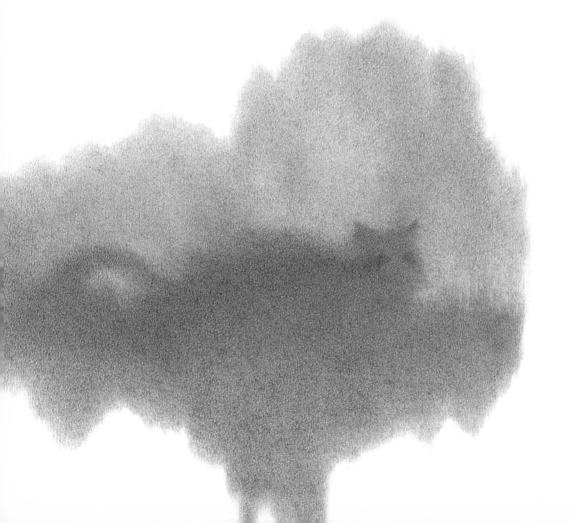

A white stripe
in the darkness,
skunk hunts
for someone
soft and slow
under a log.

The moon
slides
its bright face
into the pond.
Hello, fish!

At the tip of the pond
muskrat stops,
swallowing
the coldness,
the brightness
of stars.

Underground
a small pink star
moves, touching
blackness.

Mole is running
through her winding home.

The meadow hides secrets
in its deepest places.
Under the sky
under the grass
under the moles
under the rock
dinosaurs sleep.

Clouds
hush
the man in the moon.

A stone in the grass,
small turtle sleeps,
her first day
filling her.

Turtle
slides his old brown head
under his roof,
turning out the stars
the cloud-sliced moon.

Tonight
one hundred years
of days and nights
fit snug
inside with him.

In the meadow
a day between seasons ends
and time creeps on
making quiet changes.

On the old stone wall
flowers twist tight, goodnight,
and the first new bud
wakes, uncurls
waiting for a new day.